Uneven Lanes

poems

by

Caitlin M.S. Buxbaum

Red Sweater Press
P.O. Box 870414
Wasilla, AK 99687
caitbuxbaum.com/red-sweater-press

Copyright © 2019 Caitlin M.S. Buxbaum. All rights reserved.

Printing fulfilled by Amazon. No part of this book may be used or reproduced in any manner whatsoever without written permission of the publisher except in the case of brief quotations embodied in critical articles and reviews.

All included images are the work of the author. Cover image of Vine Road, taken three days after the Nov. 30, 2018 Alaska earthquake.

ISBN-13: 978-1-7332677-3-1
ISBN-10: 1-7332677-3-5

For Sean

Contents

|

Mothers	1
Spumoni	2
In laws	3
what if instead	4
10-4	5
Together	6
Untitled	7
Husband	8

| \

Tryst	11
Seward // London	12
Change	13
Wild	14
little things	15
Vicar	16
Tokyo > San Francisco	17

| \ |

lists	21
the 20s	22
activism/activist	23

| \ | /

Balance	27
Tchotchkes	28
Memory	30

Acknowledgments

About the Author

Uneven Lanes

I

Mothers
Spumoni
In laws
what if instead
10-4
Together
Untitled
Husband

Mothers

Nothing like
listening to a parent
discipline their child
the wrong way
to quell the maternal instinct,
or at least its manifestation;
let our fears not keep us
from becoming the mothers
we ought
or ought not
to be.

Spumoni

a garish-looking flavor
that sounds more awful
and bewildering
than it tastes; opposite
a wedding, which
sounds much lovelier
in its gaudiness than
the impossible logistics & judgments
that necessarily accompany it

at least I can vouch
for the sweetness of the man
who will be waiting
at the end of the aisle.

In laws

In my new family,
picking a song for my fiancé
and his mother to dance to
is like taking a time machine
to a non-existent era where
oldies meet sexy swing and
'90s boy bands, along with
crooning balladeers entrenched in sorrow—
an era which only came
into figurative being
when I asked my sisters-in-law
for advice.

what if instead

what if instead
of the petty arguments
many associate with marriage,
we could only recall
the times our spouses
made us feel special & loved?
not the diamond rings
or extravagant vacations,
but the hard days & sleepless nights
punctuated by an afternoon
when you had tonsillitis
and he made you chicken noodle soup;
these are the moments
I want to remember.

10-4

what was once devised
to exceed the dynamotor's spin
they say
is a thing of the past,
that the equivalent "understood"
does not guarantee understanding
at all,
with the infestation of languages
that differ too much for safety

me, I dream
the code's origin
came from a sonnet, with each line
speaking a universal tongue:
Love.
Italian or English,
it all adds up the same.

Together

for Doris and Randall Bjerken

He walks beside me
outside me
on a warm summer night
sensing me
protecting me
from any oncoming traffic
that might spiral out of control
on this quiet, wooded road

I appreciate the gesture,
but I also remember
those two paragons of virtue
lost suddenly
in an *impossible* accident,
we thought.

Maybe it doesn't matter
what comes, just that we face it
suffer it
together.

Untitled

'Marriage is easy,
but that wedding stuff, man...'
is how I remember my
new husband's words
yesterday, and before you
laugh, hear the truth
in that sarcasm, which allowed us
our relaxation;

I've heard it said "this is YOUR day"
but what most people are
not saying
is how much work the party is,
for a payoff
mostly in pictures.

Still, the choice to love
can be made, and will,
before forever begins,
and in the middle,
and at the "end."

Husband

Smells like teen spirit
Except for the
Angry-sounding parts, the
Nonsensical-seeming album cover

Perhaps he's more like
A song you've never heard
That sounds familiar
Ringing in your ears
Interminably, but not incessantly;
Calm, cool and caring, not
Known, or kept secret,

But waiting to be heard,
Unlike the Top 40s that only last the week.
X-ray his tune,
Breathe in that melody,
And sense what I sense:
Undying devotion and love
Meant only for me and Him.

|\

Tryst
Seward // London
Change
Wild
little things
Vicar
Tokyo > San Francisco

Tryst

wet, white dandelions
and an old "friend" I'd
rather not see
pass through the music
of the main attraction—
the scents of Something sweet
sparking the summer rain
with a thought you didn't dare have
until this moment

Seward // London

low tide
fog on the mountains
the (mostly) open road —
a well-timed trip south
in celebration of
90 years running
that truly iconic peak
& 240 years of freedom
from a place we love to visit
while ignoring our abhorrence
of authority
and our obsession
with ownership

Change

isn't the world a little bit more
everywhere
than it used to be, and that's why
you can't see that Good Country Woman
standing on the porch steps anymore
telling her grubby kids in their overalls
'be back by dinnertime y'all' or
'back by dark, y'hear'? Home is
bigger, smaller than before, and no,
is it less safe? But we see it that way;
this is not our playground
anymore.

Wild

You know you still live
in a wild place
when the smells
wafting in your windows
as you cruise the back streets
remind you of a quiet hamlet
rather than some industrial metropolis;
the scents of clover and lilac
running through your hair,
not diesel, oil and the manufactured...

I guess a little bit of nature
goes a long way
with minimal distraction
from reality.

little things

a conversation with a complete stranger
bad news about a pet dog
the anticipation of traveling abroad
crusty Chinese food with a fork
coming home to a napping husband
and playing pirate in the sea of foreign film
—all mixed together, order important
but not a reflection of rank—
make for an exceptional day
in an ordinary week (ignore the podcast),
and an attitude as jovial as the moon
looked on by others in the daylight

Vicar

It's watching the romance unfold
onscreen, innocently, unsullied by
gratuitousness and modernity
that gets me thinking about
quality of character, and how we
write it into existence so flawlessly
that for a moment—as many as we
observe—we believe in it,
relish it, in one sense or another;
are you wistful, hopeful, lustful,
in awe of the power of the created?
I think only of the potential,
I tell myself, but perhaps I, too,
am merely a vicarious lover.

Tokyo > San Francisco

making our descent
a beautiful distraction
the city at night

| \ |
lists
the 20s
activism/activist

lists

i live in lists, these days,
it seems, and in what ways
i'll tell: in details i don't dare
to dwell, in depth i cannot care.
avoidance is the practice of obsession,
unblinking, hidden by the stair —
it gives off a subtle scent, an air of despair.
this will not last, I tell myself in haste
 so that I keep my cluttered mind chaste —
free from responsibility
gone from the wide-eyed world
stunted by the saturated market…
but even now,
sensing my destiny.

the 20s

i have become a person
afraid of the world
in my womanhood
my youth
my religion
and even in my privilege;
in my Unfulfilled Potential
as well as my Love

fear of failure
of inadequacy
of obsolescence
of death
brings to light
something dark
that looms over my life —

i think it is called
the 20s.

activism/activist

dismantle
reassemble
threaten the current way
dominate
yes I said dominate
dominate the day
reform
break down
destroy, even, you say
fight
erase
make the System pay
when even as you
blur the lines
the answers come out gray
who then
are you
to keep ideas at bay

dismantle
reassemble
you say it's the only way
but read
your words
damn you and your day
you cannot hide
your violence
keep chanting
while I pray

| \ | /

Balance
Tchotchkes
Memory

Balance

My life is unbalanced
like the junk in the back of my car —
out of sight, out of mind
until it isn't. As the laundry and
dishes pile up, I start to feel
the guilt
the shame that drives action
sometimes

And then there are other parts of my life,
like an LP — retro, cool again, but always
presenting the listener with the
nagging sense
that it will once again go out of style,
and sit pretty, unused…
and in that lack of utility, ugly,
but irreplaceable,
or if not irreplaceable,
impossible to throw away.

So the burden grows, sometimes motivating,
sometimes dragging you down, but it
stays with you, all the same. I doubt
there's a way to get rid of it — ever.

I'm not sure I would want to.

Tchotchkes

I'm looking at my grandmother's tchotchkes,
thinking,
when she said she didn't want any more
things piling up, what she really meant was,
'I'll die soon.'
So it wasn't so much, 'I want jam for my birthday,' as
'I don't want to saddle you with more heirlooms
to parcel out after my death.'
Thoughtful,
unassuming and humble; wise, in a way
I may never understand.

But now, Grandma, those paperweights
and thingamabobs
those whozits and whatzits
are some of my most
cherished possessions.

Memory

The smell of powdered apple cider mix
brings me back to a time I
scarcely remember
and will likely forget even more
as the years are added to my life.
There's a cabin, small and clouded
by a blizzard like I have never seen
and have yet to experience since;
a blanket of white so thick
it makes you consider how long
you might be able to "hold it,"
a covering so sure
it kept our ride home at bay
for days. But it also showed me
a glimpse of micro-life, maybe not
scientifically, but positionally
as I observed that small white ermine
dipping in and out of the snow
totally comfortable
unlike me, a human in over-sized
flannel, holed up where no animal
would go, except
in the absence of us.

That cider-smelling, Top Ramen-slurping
time from my childhood, which brought
my family food for the winter
(without my assistance)
remains one of the fondest memories
of my existence.

Acknowledgments

Thanks to my family — in laws and all — for being a constant source of inspiration and support.

About the Author

Caitlin M.S. Buxbaum is a writer, teacher, photographer and coach from Wasilla, Alaska. She has a Master of Arts in Teaching from the University of Alaska Anchorage and a Bachelor of Arts in Japanese and English with an emphasis in Creative Writing from Gustavus Adolphus College. *Uneven Lanes* is her third book of poetry.

Follow the author on Facebook, Twitter & Instagram @caitbuxbaum or visit her website: caitbuxbaum.com

Other Books by Caitlin M.S. Buxbaum

Songs from the Underground

Ever Unknown, Ever Misunderstood

Wabi-Sabi World: An Artist's Search

www.ingramcontent.com/pod-product-compliance
Lightning Source LLC
Chambersburg PA
CBHW041814040426
42450CB00004B/153